SEASONS OF LOVE AR

Tamiko Dooley read Latin and French at New College, Oxford. She was the winner of the BBC Radio 3 carol competition 2021.

Also by Tamiko Dooley

SHIMA (Islands)   (Alien Buddha, 2022)

Seasons of Love Around the Rising Sun

Tamiko Dooley

Broken Sleep Books

ISBN: 978-1-915760-07-4

Cover designed by Aaron Kent

Edited & Typeset by Aaron Kent

Broken Sleep Books Ltd   Broken Sleep Books Ltd
Rhydwen   Fair View
Talgarreg   St Georges Road
Ceredigion   Cornwall
SA44 4HB   PL26 7YH

Contents

Haru (Spring)

Hanami (Viewing cherry blossom)

If I'd known that was the last time we'd meet –
Turning back, I saw you on the viewing
Platform, your palm pressed flat against the glass
Lines tracing the paths your life had taken

Narita was humming with travellers
For *hanami* and karaoke songs
Had I known that was the very last time –
I wouldn't have boarded the aeroplane

Your wrinkled face was smiling peacefully
Perhaps you knew and chose to let me go
You didn't say the petals would soon fall
That the branches would be bare in the sky

Sakura: the brevity of being,
A moment in time, captured forever.

on the Shinkansen

they call me the bullet train
        but do not calculate my worth
                in kilometres per hour, or time, or distance.
                speed is a by-product
                      of what I am.

                look under your chair,
        you'll find no specks of dust to count.
    turn to the wide window
and you'll not see glass, but
        unopoilt sky and the earth crying out for stillness.

        soon, the kanji figure of eight
            of Fuji-san, lucky number *hachi*,
                will slow your heartbeat
              as if Hokusai's hand were carving it
        in real time.
    do not seek to learn its height,
or scale its slopes,
        or preserve it in a picture.

        i move silently. close your eyes,
            and you could be in an armchair at
home.
                this quietness is what I bring
      you,
        forged by the bullet's unwavering path.

        marvel at the plains and trees and
    allow yourself to sink into these scenes.
this is a journey about you,
        outside of time and place.

Kayobi (Tuesday)

The bedtime story isn't told
Perching on the edge of his wipe-clean mattress
Or from the dinosaur beanbag
In the corner of his room.
She doesn't need to avoid the
creaky floorboard on the way out.

Instead, as his eyelids flutter
And he steals away to today and yesterday,
To what will and could be,
She peers into the screen
And watches his grip on *kuma-chan* loosen
As one by one his fingers drop.

Once his shallow breathing beats a regular rhythm,
He's *yume no naka* – in his dreams.
She stays awhile, drinking him in
From the other side of the town,
Singing *Komori-uta*, a lullaby, and brushing her
Fingers across the stuffed Totoro
He left at hers a year ago -
Only intended for a short stay, to be washed properly.
He hasn't been picked up yet.

She tries to recall the feather of his cheek,
The tickle of his overgrown mop,
His heaviness on her lap,
the scent of the soap he uses for eczema.

When the screen flickers
And she's staring into darkness,
She thinks of *Kayobi, hachi-ji*, next Tuesday, 8 o'clock,
and it wraps futon-like around her
And keeps her warm.

Baba's rice

for I will count the ways my grandmother consumes rice:

i.   Sustenance
before sunrise, she rinses and dries the grains.
a good soak prepares them for the
rice cooker. we eat it with grilled *saba* and miso soup:
our daily bread.

ii.   Skincare
she splashes her face
with the starchy water left over from
washing the rice – *as plump as a
sumo wrestler's left cheek* she hoots,
slapping her face to wake it up.

iii.   Healing
in sickness, sour plum porridge soothes my fever -
umeboshi can cure your headache Baba says,
plucking the wrinkly fruit and placing it
on my shivering forehead.

iv.   Healing II
when a fish bone jams in my throat
she tells me to scoff the rice
with a wide mouth at the brim of the bowl
to ease it down.

v. Adhesive

if we are out of glue
she uses leftover rice
to stick down the flap of an envelope.

vi. Love

when she feeds me with her chopsticks,
mouthful by mouthful,
her lips mimicking mine as I close them,
our hearts seem to beat in time together.

Tadaima (I'm home)

On the way to your house in Nakano:
I heard the slurp of salarymen as they sat at *ramen* bars
Backs hunched over bowls like blackbirds in a line

Dim lanterns from each *izakaya* guided the way to yours
They swayed in the breeze of September
As if the heat of the summer had been a dream

I knew I was coming home

My key turned in the lock and I saw you turn and smile
Your slippers were laid out, facing forwards for me to wear
So I could slip into how we used to be

I neared the kitchen, and the scent of your vegetable *tempura*
Swirled with steam from the rice cooker
Your blue apron stained with greasy handprints

I knew I was coming home

I went upstairs to change, into the *yukata* you laid out for me
Creaseless and clean, I brushed my hair and washed my face
When I came downstairs you had made *hojicha* tea

I raised the china cup to my lips and scalded them
The leaves danced in the ceramic, drifting towards me

And when your hand touched my cheek and you whispered *okaerinasai*
My face was awash with tears:

I knew I was coming home

Mukashi Mukashi (Once Upon a Time)

Listen, one day the fairy tale will save your life.

When the five year olds saw the skyline rising
Just as their grandparents had described to them
Whispered during bedtime stories
Tucked up in futons with a blue lamp flickering to
Burn the mosquitos away:

When the horizon moves, you run.

Those who hadn't remembered, hadn't paid attention
Didn't dash for high ground
They waited for the bus, the train, the taxi
It was too late by then.

But the starters and finishers of the great race
Sprinted, breathless, to elevated land together
And watched the god Susanowo unfold his arms
Unleash his fury, from a tiny tremor leagues below the Pacific

Destroying with a torrent of water / Engulfing everything

They watched as Noah from the helm of his ark:

A tale told, now turning true.

Natsu (Summer)

Susumu

The sun beat down on Tokyo intensely:
Forty-five in the shade. The *matsu* tree
Stretched out across Susumu's back garden,
Providing relief from the scorching heat.

Susumu's dad had finally convinced
Him to have the minor operation:
Yarinasai, he'd growled, *don't be a coward* –
Susumu was frightened but had no choice.

They hadn't expected his reaction
To the anaesthetic on the table.
Samurais fall on swords than show weakness:
The old Lie was exposed and the old man
Wept under the branches shading his face
From the fire that watched Icarus fall.

Kokeshi doll

Uncle Hiroshi came to visit one airless summer evening:
Charcoal, cigarette-stained suit; oversized, amber glasses
And greasy strands held in place over an
Ostrich egg's head.

He was clutching a wooden kokeshi doll
Garish lips and unlidded eyes delicately painted on.
Iroke, sex appeal, of a geisha
For my chubby five-year-old hands.

She squeaks when you turn her head
he croaked, bending over me,
Gold molar glinting in a graveyard of jagged tombstones
And a fog of ashen breath.

His gyoza fingers gripped the head and forced it back and forth.
She's mute at first, and he holds his breath with the effort
Of twisting the neck:
Wood grinding on wood.

She's silent; face inert, fringe still
Shoulders hunched in protest.
Eventually, she makes a sound.
See, he snickers, *you just have to push it harder.*

In the distance, I hear the minor third of ambulance sirens,
Young cries for help in the suffocating night.

Umeboshi

It nestles in the corner of my *ekiben*, my bento box from the station.

Umeboshi: they let you know first when it's time to pick them:

Hard pink nipples hammering down on the copper roof,
　　　clogging gutters and scaring our cat Toto - both in season.

Ume, then - still unripe, unsweetened plum, packed as commuters
from Ikebukuro
　　　to Shinjuku in glass cases
　　　　　(Some ladies-only to stop the fondling. Nothing fond about it.)

We place them under the slats of hand-tied tatami straw flooring
　　　Remember that boy from school who'd ask about shibari with a smile?

In darkness, during the year, they rub up and against each other,
　　　Leaking juices, and spreading their sweetness

　　　　　-　slippery when wet says the platform sign　-

　But who knows what happens underground?

Until it's made its way here, dried, a sour tang to my lunchbox,
　　　before I board the train.

Nemawashi (Around the Roots)

Do you remember that stifling summer,
When they resurfaced our street, in Higashi Nakano?
Slabs were outdated; tarmac was in.
The acers growing on the verges
Observed silently as the residents and council
Bickered over who owned the land, and who had to pay.
Eventually the prefecture of Tokyo stumped up the cash.

Plans were made, timetables set;
The trees permitted to stay, untouched.
There would be one irksome week
Where we couldn't park outside our homes –
Cars and lives uprooted for a while.

Then the diggers came: gigantic flashing monsters
Mining the lane, hi-vis vehicles that
Swirled and dumped piles of smoking tar.
It was deposited and levelled carefully
Until the plastic smell of pitch
Permeated every *futon* hung on balconies
To absorb sunlight for a good night's sleep.

Red triangular signs warned us of the stickiness,
The *sawaranai* – no touching for seventy-two hours.
Pedestrians danced up and down ramps and
Around cones, avoiding the candy cane tape
All for the new road – a gleaming black marvel to behold.

Plenty of effort, worth the pain.
We'd be able to walk whilst using our phones
And cycle without jolts to our joints.
We clapped ourselves on the back
For a job well done, a smooth surface laid with relative ease.

It was only a few weeks later
Tiny cracks began to appear, imperceptibly,
Traces of tremors from below:

The maples, until then tacit bystanders
Began disrupting the even earth –
First an arm, then a leg,
Interrupting our commutes and conversations
Our *Konichiwa! Genki?*
With thick limbs breaking through,
Forcing their way towards the light and
Shattering the ground we had laid.

Whilst we had been quarrelling amongst ourselves
The true proprietors of the soil reminded us
Of their presence, we were mere trespassers.

They were taking their vengeance:
shizen no kataki uchi

And their voices were going to be heard.

Shi'ppe gaishi (Unexpected vengeance)

after Virgil's Georgics, book ii

That July, a group of us went camping in the fields
Behind our summer cabin in Nagano, where the
Yuzu and *kaki* trees grew freely and the great *matsu*
Offered its branches for swings.

On our inaugural expedition
We marched in a line to the open plain
Down the long, narrow path where nettles grew on either side,
Careful not to brush our shins against them.
Turtle-like, we bore equipment on our backs:
Stove and tents, sleeping bags and lanterns,
Beef curry to cook over an open fire.

Ants scattered, losing their column formations
As we upturned logs for seating;
The birds, disturbed, flew portentously as when
Romulus perceived them overhead.
We boisterously collected twigs and foliage
To deploy our own nest, to mark out boundary lines.

After a raucous evening creating shelter and a hot meal,
With bellies full we fell asleep to the
Tune of *korogi*, crickets, and a solitary owl.

In the morning, as we packed up, deep holes remained
Where we had brandished pegs into the soft, inviting earth.
The previously luscious grass was straw-like
Where the tent had been pitched.

As we stamped out the last of the flames
Ash flew into the morning sky
Scenting the leaves above us with charcoal.

A shallow trench blackened with broken and burnt wood
Remained a marker of our success.

Bleary-eyed, our cohort headed towards home
And suddenly halted –
Had the nettles grown taller overnight?
The pathway rippled with gleams of steel,
An array of javelins facing towards and over us
Sharp blades pointing, accusing us of invasion of their territory.

As we bowed our heads in apology
And passed the ranks of verdant daggers
They continued to close in on us:
The further we went, the closer they crept
Forcing us to shield bare legs and arms from the incoming attack.

That summer, when we turned fifteen,
We learned that respect, *sonkei*, was not just for grown-ups.

We had disturbed their habitat and our punishment was nigh.

Tombo (Dragonflies)

At Myo-onji shrine in Tokyo
The dragonflies dance around my head

We're here to place Grandad's ashes into the family burial site
The September breeze rises and falls, and rises again
I hold a photograph in my hand, faded and folded

When they placed Grandad in his coffin
They removed the picture of me from his wallet
So he wouldn't pull me over to the other side

In the picture, I'm a gap-toothed six-year-old next to Taro the dog
Although if he was still with us, perhaps I'm five
It was a warm late summer day when Grandad took the photograph
We had planned an adventure in the hills of Nagano
To hunt dragonflies and eat our *omusubi* rice balls by the lake
The *tombo* swarmed thickly around us
We caught them in our long-necked nets to study them in giant
glass jars

At sunset Grandad said it was time to release them
Everything belongs back where it comes from
Taro barked as they flew into the peach-red sky
They mingled with the fireflies, just then beginning to enflame the
evening

I hold this picture in my hand
And as the monk pours the grey dust and chants a prayer

The dragonflies dance around my head

Aki (Autumn)

Signs

We came for the *soba* noodles
But they stick to the bottom of the bowl
The spider crabs crawl peacefully over Mibaru beach
Unaware of the storm that's rising over the ocean
When we board the boat, I wave to a whale
I'd read that they respond to signals
Sure enough it comes up starboard
Splashing and spraying us from its blowhole
I say that I asked the whale to join us
You don't respond
Perhaps the salty air carried my words away
The trip to Okinawa only began this morning
It's already clear
We came for the *soba* noodles
But they stick to the bottom of the bowl

Wagamama

Perhaps I could have picked a better place to tell him –
your food won't arrive at the same time
I've been trying to end things since December
because we bring it when it's ready
I'm not sure if he knows or not
can I get you guys a drink?
Although we haven't touched each other for months
maybe a green tea?
So perhaps he hasn't noticed
are you ready to order now?
The benches are rather close together
great choice!
I'm elbowing the people either side of me
just to remind you
I'll have to say it quietly
your food won't arrive
But firmly
at the same time
At least we're in public
because we bring the food
So he can't lash out at me
when it's ready

Back when I was little
My mother would call me *wagamama*:
Spoilt, selfish, naughty

Did she mean it, or was she foreshadowing this
here's your katsu curry
Very
and your miso soup
Moment
can I get you anything else?

Sayaka

They made her change her name –
The same *kanji* she'd used since she first picked up a pencil
To mark on paper. *Sayaka.*

The fortune teller said it was bad luck
For the characters of his surname to mix with hers.
What's in a name, they'd taught her in Shakespeare class.
She was becoming his wife, after all.

When she was stamping the documents to change it,
She paused. *It will still read the same,*
The man at the desk had laughed. *Just the kanji is different.*

Somewhere inside, tectonic plates were shifting,
Distant rumblings threatening to erupt,
Calling her *Sayaka*, written the way it was supposed to be,
The way it had been since she was born.

Yurushi (Forgiveness)

Last night I dreamt of you:
You were turned away as we spoke
I couldn't see your face

You were kneeling on the floor
Facing the *fusuma* door as it slid shut
Closing on all my mistakes

I heard your voice, as rough as the scales of salmon
You'd grab with yellow rubber gloves
As she swam upstream

I felt the brush of your shoulder
As I reached for you to explain
But you didn't move

I tasted the bitter dregs of *hojicha* tea
Left to brew all evening

And when my forehead touched the *tatami* floor in apology
You were turned away

I couldn't see your face

Gochiso-sama (Thank you for the meal)

I wait for you to raise your chopsticks first
As you insist

Steam from the bowl of miso soup clouds your face
You slurp it up loudly

I don't know how to tell you

The seaweed sticks in my throat
Clam shells release their sand, gritty between my teeth

You turn to pour more hot water into the teapot
The *genmaicha* leaves brew for a second time

I booked my train ticket

We eat in silence as usual
Without our eyes meeting

The skin of the grilled *saba* fish crackles
As you snap it in half and remove the spine

One-way from Tokyo to Sendai

From next door, I hear the sound of children

I cannot tell whether they are laughing or crying

Fuyu (Winter)

Noodle's Revenge

Each New Year's Day we celebrated with a
Bowl of noodle soup at Aunt Hideko's house.
My sister and I, dolled-up in our scarlet and gold kimonos,
Would twinkle across town in our geta shoes
To join the family feast and welcome good fortune for the year ahead.

The longer the noodles, the longer the life!
The louder the slurp, the more grateful the mouth!

Cousins, aunties and uncles swigged and sucked the unruly strings
Swallowed in large greedy gulps,
Stretchy and loud with their pops and slaps,
Taming them with a smack of the lips and a glug of sweet broth.

In the afternoon we would loosen our obi belts
And recline on the tatami floor, bellies full and jaws battle-weary,
Ready to listen to the wireless replay classic enka songs.

Then one bitterly cold January,
We arrived early at the gathering. The house was silent, yet
From round the back
We heard shrieks and breathless gasps.
Concerned, we crept to the garden gate and spotted
O, horror! In all directions the
Hairy toes and scrawny knees of aunties,
Nightdresses raised to reveal
White lacy bloomers waving in the freezing air –
Hair wild, gums grinning, naked feet
Stamping out a New Year's rhythm on the virgin-white dough.
Aunt Hideko stomped and roared as her
Wrinkled, flaking feet kneaded and clawed at the sticky white substance
Destined to be our lunch.

The stronger the legs, the tastier the noodles!

I turned, wretched and retching. They had shown their true nature
And I knew that if I stayed they would deal another blow:
A strike of my cheeks, a swift wrap around my neck
And with one firm swipe pull me into their hellish soup.

Mizu (Water)

I wrote the *kanji* of your name
In water on a paving stone

Each brushstroke a prayer to heal you
The sun stole the first letter before I finished

It was impossible to compose your name in full
Even when I raced through it

Life: one second within the stretches of time
A droplet that splashes, stains and fades

Ending almost as soon as it begins

Choices (Erabu)

If I dream of you,
I steal you into my mind,
Or you choose to come?

yume no naka
kimi o sarauka
kimi ga kuru?

Sayonara

I saw you from the waiting room
Through the glass window
Leading to the white ward
You tipped your hat to say *sayonara*

We were sitting on wicker chairs
With the faded pink cushions
Staring at the minute-hand and waiting
For Dr Tanaka to give us some news

That was when you strolled down the corridor
Clad in your finest three-piece suit
Tweed waistcoat, trilby and umbrella
Your hair jet-black, its former hue

After five nights' stay
The nurses had been so kind to us
We knew it couldn't be long

You paused by my chair and smiled
I saw you consult your pocket watch
The gold chain swung gently
You turned to leave through the double doors

When Dr Tanaka approached
Ushered by two nurses with heads bowed
I knew what he was going to say

I saw you from the waiting room

You tipped your hat to say *sayonara*

Eki (The Station)

I was sitting on the station platform when I saw you
You were standing in the last carriage of the train
Tozai line, heading eastwards

A newspaper in one hand, the other holding the strap
The ones I used to reach for where you would lift me up
Letting me dangle for a second, little legs kicking the air

When the train jolted and stopped at Otemachi station
I looked up from my book to check if it was my train
That's when our eyes met

It was hard to tell if it was you at first
You smiled slowly and I recognised
The creases in your face that I see in the mirror today

It made sense to see you on your daily commute, only natural

The doors stayed open
A sudden breeze rushed across the platform between us
A deep breath and release

You nodded at me slowly

The whistle blew so loudly I dropped my bookmark
When I stooped to pick it up the train had started moving

I didn't see you leave

I ran to catch up but the train
Was diminishing into the distance

That was when the stone in my chest began to lighten a little

When I knew it was time to open up and let go
Stop chasing, move forward

I was sitting on the platform

You were standing in the carriage

Shogi no taikai (Chess match)

If I tell you of the *ohmisoka*, the New Year's Eve
Where you gave me the hardwood *shogi* set
Would you remember that year?

Each piece was hand-carved with delicate *kanji*
The underside of the grid board
Green velvet: no slips.

If I gave you the bishop to hold in your hand
Could you tell me which way he moves?

It was a stormy night at our house in Higashi Nakano
My parents and I were up late listening to the radio
Slurping our *soba* noodles as old *enka* songs played quietly

The doorbell rang unexpectedly
Clashing shrilly with the minor key
You burst into our hallway, throwing off your shoes

You ran to me and swept me up
I inhaled the smoky undertones of your aftershave
And your shampoo – a heady mixture.

When I opened the *shogi* set that year
You taught me about life:
Rules and routes and hierarchy
Black and white, winning and losing.

When you came round to visit
We would play it together
And you'd lose every time.

I never knew you chose to let me win.

You might not remember my name today
But I tell you of that evening
And the way you always made me feel

I place a pawn in your fist
And I clutch your hands tightly
To hold on to you and to show you I'm here

That it isn't checkmate
Not even check –

We will learn the laws of this new game, this new world you inhabit
We will not give up on each other

And this time we will both win.

Heat, transferring

She peeks in the window.

He's busy; surrounded by colourful bricks.
Inside it's warm, and the fire keeps out the
Cold January frost.

He spots her and beams -
And rushes to the pane.
He knows by now he can't dash to the door.

Two hands meet on the glass –
Hers: shrivelled, wrinkly and well-worn
The hand that fed, clothed and bathed me;
His: chubby and pen-stained, still
Alternately clinging to my legs and pounding the floor in frustration.

For a moment the world stops,
And these two souls, two sides of me
Collide. Gently.
She tells him silently
How much she misses him,
And he does the same.

The icy glass begins to warm under their palms
Until it's time for her to leave,
To stay safe,

To stay apart.

Long after she's gone,
The handprint remains there,
As warm and comforting as the promise of Spring
And brighter times to come.

Acknowledgements

A huge "arigato" to Aaron and the Broken Sleep team for choosing to publish my poems. To the reader: thank you for picking up this book - I hope my work resonates with you.

LAY OUT YOUR UNREST